SLIP STREA

GREATEST ROCK
BANDS

ANNE ROONEY

First published in 2012 by
Franklin Watts
338 Euston Road
London NW1 3BH

Franklin Watts Australia
Level 17/207 Kent Street
Sydney NSW 2000

© Franklin Watts 2012

(pb) ISBN: 978 1 4451 1359 3
(library ebook) ISBN: 978 1 4451 2446 9

Dewey Classification number: 428.6

Series Editors: Adrian Cole and Jackie Hamley
Series Advisors: Diana Bentley and Dee Reid
Series Designer: Peter Scoulding
Picture Researcher: Diana Morris

Printed in China

Franklin Watts is a division of
Hachette Children's Books,
an Hachette UK company.
www.hachette.co.uk

Acknowledgements:
Alamy Celebrity/Alamy: 22b.
Bill Cross/Associated Newspapers/Rex
Features: 13. Deymos/Shutterstock: 17.
dwphotos/Shutterstock: 4-5b, 8b, 12b,
16b, 20b. Anton Gvozdikov/Shutterstock:
front cover. Hulton Archive/Getty Images:
9. Jeff Kravitz/Film Magic/Getty Images:
5bl, 21. Frank Micelotta/Getty Images:
20c. vardin nardin/Shutterstock: 22t.
Northfoto/Shutterstock: 4cl, 6b. Terry
O'Neill /Getty Images: 7t. David Redfern/
Getty Images: 5tl, 16c. Brian J Richie/
Hotsauce/Rex Fetaures: 5br, 23. Henry
Ruggeri/Corbis: 5tr, 19. Ray Stevenson/
Rex Features: 4cr, 10b, 11, 12c. Peter
Still/Getty Images: 14b, 15. David Thorpe/
Rex Features: 1, 18b. Marius Wegan/
Shutterstock: 8c.

Every attempt has been made to
clear copyright. Should there be any
inadvertent omission, please apply
to the publisher for rectification.

CONTENTS

GREATEST ROCK BANDS

Fans go mad for their favourite rock bands! Which is your favourite?

Here are six of the greatest rock bands.

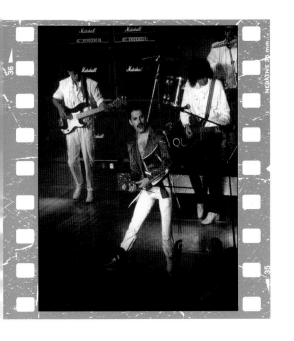

THE ROLLING STONES

The Rolling Stones formed in the UK in 1962.

They still play today. They have made 29 albums.

The lead singer of the Rolling Stones
is called Mick Jagger.

He is famous for his
mad dancing.

THE WHO

The Who formed in the UK in 1964.

The Who were famous for smashing guitars. They still play today.

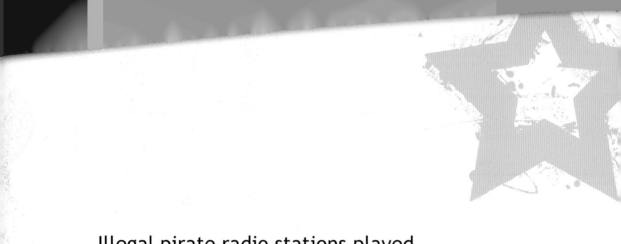

Illegal pirate radio stations played their music. The most famous pirate station was Radio Caroline. It was on a ship.

QUEEN

Queen formed in the UK in 1971.
They made the first music video in 1975.

Queen did one of the best-ever rock
shows. It was at Live Aid in 1985.

Their lead singer was called Freddie Mercury. He died in 1991.

There is a stage show about Queen. It is called "We Will Rock You".

AC/DC

AC/DC were formed by two brothers.
They formed in Australia in 1973.
AC/DC were the first big heavy metal band.

Their most famous album is "Back in Black".
It is the third best-selling album ever.

NIRVANA

Nirvana were the first big grunge band.
They formed in the USA in 1987.
Nirvana used soft and loud sounds.

Their lead singer was called Kurt Cobain.
He died in 1994. Then the band split up.

ARCTIC MONKEYS

Arctic Monkeys formed in the UK in 2002.
Fans put their music on the internet.
Arctic Monkeys were soon famous!

They made the fastest-selling debut
album in the UK. It was called "Whatever
People Say I am, That's What I'm Not."
It was made in 2006.

INDEX

FOR TEACHERS

About SLIPSTREAM

Slipstream is a series of expertly levelled books designed for pupils who are struggling with reading. Its unique three-strand approach through fiction, graphic fiction and non-fiction gives pupils a rich reading experience that will accelerate their progress and close the reading gap.

At the heart of every Slipstream non-fiction book is exciting information. Easily accessible words and phrases ensure that pupils both decode and comprehend, and the topics really engage older struggling readers.

Whether you're using Slipstream Level 1 for Guided Reading or as an independent read, here are some suggestions:

1. Make each reading session successful. Talk about the text before the pupil starts reading. Introduce any unfamiliar vocabulary.

2. Encourage the pupil to talk about the book using a range of open questions. For example, what is their favourite rock band and why?

3. Discuss the differences between reading non-fiction, fiction and graphic fiction. What do they prefer?

For guidance, SLIPSTREAM Level 1 – Greatest Rock Bands has been approximately measured to:

National Curriculum Level: 2c
Reading Age: 7.0–7.6
Book Band: Turquoise

ATOS: 2.0
Guided Reading Level: H
Lexile® Measure (confirmed): 380L

Slipstream Level photocopiable **WORKBOOK**
ISBN: 978 1 4451 1609 9
available – download free sample worksheets from:
www.franklinwatts.co.uk